Law Enforcement

Customs Service

by Michael Green

Content Consultant:
Donald F. Beach
Attorney
The U.S. Customs Service (retired)

RiverFront Books

An Imprint of Franklin Watts
A Division of Grolier Publishing
New York   London   Hong Kong   Sydney
Danbury, Connecticut

RiverFront Books
http://publishing.grolier.com

Library of Congress Cataloging-in-Publication Data
Green, Michael, 1952-
    Customs Service/by Michael Green.
    p. cm. -- (Law enforcement)
    Includes bibliographical references and index.
    Summary: An introduction to the United States Customs Service, its history, functions, responsibilities, and targeted criminals.
    ISBN 1-56065-756-1
    1. U.S. Customs Service--Juvenile literature. 2. Customs administration--United States--Juvenile literature. 3. Smuggling--United States--Juvenile literature. [1. U.S. Customs Service. 2. Smuggling.] I. Title. II. Series: Green, Michael, 1952- Law enforcement.

HJ6622.G73 1998
352.4'48'0973--dc21

                                              97-41405
                                                CIP
                                                 AC

Special thanks to the U.S. Customs Service for its help with this book.
Editorial credits:
Editor, Timothy Larson; cover design, Timothy Halldin; photo research, Michelle L. Norstad
Photo/Illustration credits:
Archive Photos/Gilbert Stuart, 8
Michael Green,15
Steve C. Healy, 18, 41
The U.S. Customs Service, cover, 4, 6, 10, 12, 16, 20, 23, 24, 26, 28, 30, 33, 34, 36, 38, 47

Table of Contents

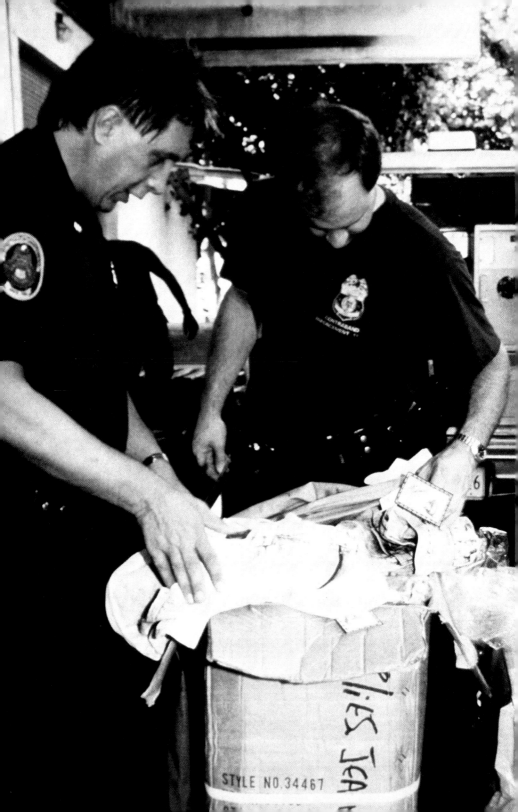

Chapter 1

The Customs Service

The U.S. Customs Service is part of the U.S. Department of the Treasury. The Treasury keeps and manages the government's money. The Customs Service enforces federal customs laws. Enforce means to make sure that laws are obeyed.

Customs laws control goods entering and leaving the United States. The laws say which goods are legal and which goods are illegal. The laws also set tariffs on goods. A tariff is a tax on goods entering a country.

Illegal goods include many things. They may include weapons, stolen art, or drugs. They might be plants or animals that can hurt the environment

Customs Service officers enforce federal customs laws.

Some illegal goods are those for which no tariff has been paid.

or spread sickness. They could be rare plants and animals that should be left in the wild.

Some illegal goods are counterfeit goods. Counterfeit goods are fake goods made to look like the real thing. Other illegal goods are goods for which no tariff has been paid.

Today's Customs Service traces its history back to the beginning of the United States. The Customs Service was the first federal law enforcement agency. A law enforcement agency is an office or department that makes sure people obey laws.

The Tariff Act

The U.S. government had little money at the end of the Revolutionary War (1776-1783). It did not have enough money to run the country. It could not afford a military force to protect its citizens. The government needed to raise money.

Congress came up with one way to raise money. Congress is the part of government that makes laws for the entire country. Congress felt the U.S. government should collect tariffs on goods coming into the country.

In 1789, Congress passed the Tariff Act. The Tariff Act allowed the U.S. government to collect tariffs on foreign products. Foreign means from another country. President George Washington signed the Tariff Act and made it law.

The Fifth Act

The U.S. government needed an agency to enforce its new tariff law. On July 31, 1789, Congress passed the Fifth Act. This act allowed the government to form the U.S. Customs

President George Washington appointed the first 99 Customs Service officers.

Service. President Washington agreed with the act and signed it into law.

President Washington appointed the first 99 Customs Service officers. The officers served at the harbors and along the borders of the original 13 states. They enforced and collected tariffs on foreign goods.

Customs Service Revenue

In its first year, the Customs Service collected $2 million in revenue. Revenue is money raised from tariffs and other taxes. The Customs Service remained the government's main source of revenue until 1913.

The Customs Service revenue helped the United States grow. It financed the Lewis and Clark Expedition. Lewis and Clark explored the area between the Mississippi River and the Pacific Ocean. Customs revenue financed the purchase of the Oregon and Louisiana Territories. It also funded the purchase of the areas that are now Florida and Alaska.

Customs Service revenue helped the U.S. government fund building projects across the country. The money financed roads, railroad lines, and buildings. It also helped the government maintain the things it built. Maintain means to keep something in good condition.

Today, the Customs Service is the government's second biggest source of revenue. It collects more than $20 billion each year.

U.S. CUSTOMS
POLICE

Chapter 2

Customs Officers

Nearly 19,000 officers work for the U.S. Customs Service today. Customs Service officers help prevent illegal goods from entering and leaving the country. They watch U.S. borders, capture smugglers, and collect illegal goods. A smuggler is a person who sneaks illegal goods into or out of a country.

There are three main kinds of customs officers. There are inspectors, canine enforcement officers, and agents. An inspector is a person who checks or searches things. An agent is a high-ranking law enforcement officer. Each kind of Customs Service officer has a special job to do.

Nearly 19,000 officers work for the U.S. Customs Service today.

Customs inspectors check anything that may contain illegal goods.

Customs Service Inspectors

Customs Service inspectors help control what enters and leaves the country. It is a difficult job. Thousands of vehicles carry tons of freight into the United States each year. A vehicle is something in which people and goods are carried. Vehicles include cars, trucks, ships, and planes. Millions of people also carry goods and property across U.S. borders each year. Most of the freight and goods are legal. But sometimes they are illegal.

Inspectors search for illegal freight and goods at ports of entry. A port of entry is a controlled place where people and goods enter a country. A port of entry can be an airport, a train station, a harbor, or a border crossing.

Inspectors check anything that may contain illegal goods. They check boxes, crates, shipping containers, baggage, and sometimes people. A shipping container is a large metal box that holds freight. Inspectors check cars, trucks, planes, boats, and trains. Inspectors have the power to seize illegal goods. They can also question and arrest people they believe are smugglers.

Canine Enforcement Officers

Canine enforcement officers work with detector dogs. Detector dogs help officers find hidden illegal goods. The dogs detect goods by following scents. Detect means to notice or discover something. Most Customs Service dogs are Labrador retrievers.

Detector dogs have a powerful sense of smell. Their sense of smell is up to 800 times more sensitive than that of humans. They can detect the scents of many goods, including drugs and explosives. Detector dogs can often smell scents through sealed packages. They can often detect goods that are in vehicles, baggage, crates, and shipping containers.

Each canine detection team includes an officer and a dog. One team can search 500 packages in 30 minutes. Or it can search one car in two minutes. An officer working alone needs more than seven days to check 500 packages. An officer needs at least 20 minutes to check a car.

Customs Service Agents

Customs Service agents look into customs crimes. There are three kinds of agents. There are special agents, air interdiction officers, and marine enforcement agents. Each kind of agent has the power to conduct searches and seize property. They also can question suspects and make arrests. A suspect is a person believed to have committed a crime.

Special agents are like police detectives. They investigate individuals, gangs of smugglers, and international companies. Investigate means gathering facts to discover who committed a crime. Some special agents investigate other

Dogs can often smell scents through sealed packages.

Customs Service officers. These agents make sure Customs Service officers obey the law while performing their jobs.

Air interdiction officers use aircraft to patrol U.S. borders. Interdiction is the act of stopping an illegal activity. The officers locate and stop air and ground smuggling operations. They pursue and capture smugglers. Some air interdiction officers are pilots.

15

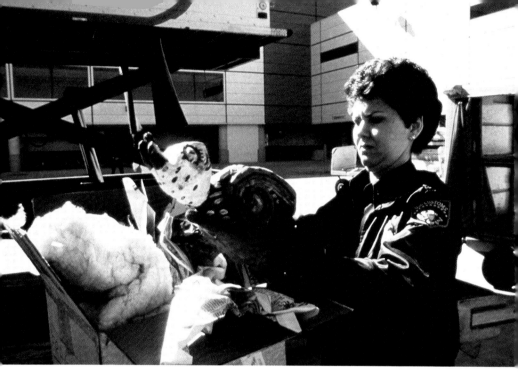

Inspectors learn how to search packages during their training.

Marine enforcement agents watch for smugglers who smuggle goods and drugs by boat. They patrol waters that form U.S. borders. These waters include oceans along the United States' southern, eastern, and western coasts. Other waters are the rivers and lakes that form part of the country's northern border.

Training

People interested in becoming Customs Service officers must complete training programs. Agent trainees attend two eight-week programs. A trainee is a person in training. Inspector trainees attend an 11-week program. Canine enforcement officer trainees and their dogs go through a 15-week program.

Agent trainees go through the Criminal Investigators Training Program first. They learn about federal laws and evidence. Evidence is facts or objects that help prove guilt. They also learn how to use weapons and how to stay alive in risky situations.

Successful agent trainees advance to the Customs Basic Enforcement Program. They learn about customs laws and ways to enforce them. They also learn how to conduct undercover operations and border-control operations. Undercover means secret.

Inspector trainees receive inspector basic training. They learn how to search packages, vehicles, ships, and planes. They also learn how to search and arrest people.

Canine enforcement trainees receive basic training in inspection and dog handling. They learn about their duties and about detector dogs. Trainees and their dogs work at becoming teams. They learn how to search for illegal goods together.

違反者は起訴される。
WARNUNG
Zuwiderhandelnde werden strafrechtlich verfolgt.
CASHIER
US Customs
Inspection Lane
Remain Behind Green Line
Until Summoned By Officer

Chapter 3

Customs Operations

Many people are familiar with the duties Customs Service inspectors perform. Travelers see inspectors check baggage at airports and other ports of entry.

Customs Service officers perform many other duties as well. Agents and officers protect importers' goods against theft. An importer is a person or company that brings legal goods into a country.

Customs Service operations protect the U.S. government against customs fraud. Customs fraud is attempting to avoid payment of tariffs. But anti-smuggling operations are the Customs Service's most important operations.

Travelers often see Customs Service inspectors at airports and other ports of entry.

Some people called mounted inspectors Customs cowboys.

Customs Cowboys

The Customs Service's earliest anti-smuggling operations took place in the original 13 states. Customs Service officers worked to stop smugglers and pirates along the East Coast. They also enforced interstate tariffs. Interstate tariffs are taxes on goods traded between states.

Anti-smuggling operations expanded as the country grew. In 1853, the Customs Service formed a group of officers who rode on horses. The Customs Service called the inspectors mounted inspectors. Some people called them Customs cowboys. Mounted inspectors protected the United States' southern border. They worked to stop the smuggling of guns, drugs, cattle, and other goods.

Mounted inspectors had a difficult job. They patrolled many miles during the day. At night, they cooked, ate, and slept outdoors. The government provided them with few supplies and little pay. The inspectors bought their own guns and clothes. They bought their own horses, saddles, and feed. Early mounted inspectors received just $2.50 per day.

Cars replaced horses during the 1920s. The Customs Service did not need as many mounted inspectors. Some inspectors continued to patrol border areas with no roads. But by 1948 there was no need for mounted inspectors. Many mounted inspectors retired. Others took different jobs within the Customs Service.

Drug Smuggling Operations

Drug smuggling has been a problem for the United States since the 1800s. But the problem did not become severe until the 1960s. Today, drug smuggling is one of the Customs Service's main concerns.

Inspectors and agents work together to stop illegal drugs from entering the United States. Inspectors check baggage, automobiles, property, and people for drugs. Canine enforcement officers work with their dogs to find drugs. Agents investigate drug smuggling cases. They arrest those who are trying to smuggle drugs.

Some special agents work undercover in other countries. Undercover agents spy on drug smuggling gangs. They gather information about the drug smugglers' activities.

Undercover agents try to find out how smugglers hide and ship drugs. They also try to discover where smugglers move drugs across U.S. borders.

Special Response Teams

Sometimes special agents work on risky operations. These operations involve smugglers who have weapons. Armed smugglers may attempt to kill the agents.

Special agents form small commando groups to deal with armed smugglers. A commando

Agents arrest people who try to smuggle drugs.

group is a heavily armed assault team. The Customs Service's commando teams are called Special Response Teams (SRTs).

Special Response Teams make raids on the armed smugglers' hideouts. A raid is a sudden and rapid assault. SRTs secure the hideouts. This means they arrest suspects and collect evidence.

Sometimes Special Response Teams need help with anti-drug smuggling operations. The Drug

Officers at the Domestic Air Interdiction Coordination Center control the Customs Service's radar.

Enforcement Administration (DEA) often provides this help. The DEA is a federal agency that works on many crimes involving drugs. The DEA sends officers to work with the Special Response Teams.

Sting Operations
Sometimes Customs Service agents perform sting operations to catch smugglers. A sting operation

is a plan of action carried out to catch smugglers in illegal activity.

Agents work undercover during a sting operation. They pretend to be buyers of smuggled goods. Sometimes agents fool smugglers. The smugglers sell shipments of smuggled goods to the agents. Then the agents arrest the smugglers and seize their goods.

The DAICC

The Domestic Air Interdiction Coordination Center (DAICC) is a command center. Customs Service officers at the center control air operations. The DAICC is located at March Air Reserve Base in California.

Officers at the center also control the Customs Service's air and ground radar. Radar is machinery that sends out radio waves to locate and guide things. Radar helps Customs Service agents spot smugglers' cars, trucks, boats, and planes.

The Customs Service has radar systems on the ground. These systems let agents monitor large areas. Monitor means to watch closely. The Customs Service also has smaller radar systems in its aircraft and on its boats. These systems cover areas that are beyond the range of ground systems.

Chapter 4

Aircraft and Boats

Until 1968, U.S. Customs Service officers had a difficult time patrolling borders. The Customs Service could not afford the aircraft and boats its officers needed. In 1968, Congress increased the amount of money it provided to the Customs Service.

Today, the Customs Service has money for modern aircraft and boats. It can now equip its aircraft and boats with the newest detection systems. These systems include radar and infrared. An infrared system is machinery that detects objects by the heat they give off.

Today, the Customs Service has the money it needs for modern aircraft.

Aerostats carry radar systems that detect objects in the air and on the ground.

Aerostats

Aerostats are large, radar-carrying balloons filled with helium. Helium is a gas that is lighter than air. Most aerostats are 230 feet (69 meters) long.

Aerostats float 10,000 to 15,000 feet (3,000 to 4,500 meters) above the ground. They are connected to the ground by long cables. A cable is a heavy wire.

Aerostats let Customs Service officers at the DAICC monitor certain places along borders. The Aerostats' radar systems detect objects in air around them. The systems also detect objects on the ground.

Customs Service Radar Plane

The Lockheed Airborne Early Warning (AEW) plane is one of the Customs Service's most important aircraft. The AEW carries an advanced radar system. Air interdiction officers use the AEW to patrol land and sea borders.

The AEW's radar system has a large rotating dish. This dish is the part of the system that sends out and receives radio waves. The dish is 24 feet (7.2 meters) wide. It is visible on top of the plane. The AEW's radar can cover an area as large as some small states.

The AEW is a four-engine plane with a top speed of 380 miles (612 kilometers) per hour. It has a range of 4,600 miles (7,406 kilometers). An airplane's range is the distance it can fly before it needs fuel. The AEW carries a crew of seven agents.

Customs Service agents use helicopters to chase and capture smugglers.

Short-Range Chase Planes

Sometimes customs agents use aircraft to chase smugglers and force them to the ground. Customs Service agents use two types of planes for short-range chase operations.

The Cessna Citation is the larger of the two planes. The Citation has two jet engines. It can fly up to 460 miles (741 kilometers) per hour. The plane has a range of 1,300 miles (2,093 kilometers).

The Citation carries radar and infrared detection systems. Agents use infrared systems at night. The systems help agents follow planes, automobiles, and even people.

The Customs High Endurance Tracker (CHET) is the second short-range chase plane. The CHET has two turbo-prop engines. A turbo-prop engine is a jet engine that turns a propeller.

The CHET's top speed is 365 miles (588 kilometers) per hour. It has a range of 800 miles (1,288 kilometers). Like the Citation, the CHET carries radar and infrared detection systems.

Helicopters

Sometimes customs agents use helicopters for short-range and long-range operations. The helicopters let agents fly into places that planes cannot reach. Helicopters can also land quickly and easily. These features make helicopters useful to agents.

The Customs Service uses American Eurocopters for short-range operations. Eurocopters have single jet engines. They have top speeds of 178 miles (287 kilometers) per hour. Each Eurocopter carries two agents and has a range of 400 miles (644 kilometers). Each Eurocopter also carries an infrared detection system.

Customs Service agents use Blackhawk helicopters for long-range operations. Blackhawk helicopters have two jet engines. The helicopters reach top speeds of 210 miles (338 kilometers) per hour. Blackhawks have a range of up to 700 miles (1,127 kilometers).

Interceptor Boats

The Customs Service uses two kinds of speedboats. Both kinds are interceptors. An interceptor is a speedboat built to catch and stop other boats. Interceptors help customs officers chase smugglers who travel in speedboats.

The Midnight Express is one kind of Customs Service interceptor. Two to three armed marine enforcement officers operate each of these boats.

Midnight Express interceptors are 37 feet (11 meters) long. They have four large engines and reach top speeds of 55 knots. A knot is a measurement of speed for ships and boats. One knot equals 1.15 miles (1.85 kilometers) per hour.

Fountain Lightning interceptors can reach speeds up to 70 knots.

Midnight Express interceptors have a range of 1,000 miles (1,610 kilometers).

The Fountain Lightning is the second kind of interceptor. Fountain Lightning interceptors come in two sizes. Some are 42 feet (12.6 meters) long. Others are 47 feet (14 meters) long. They can reach speeds up to 70 knots and cover a range of 300 miles (483 kilometers).

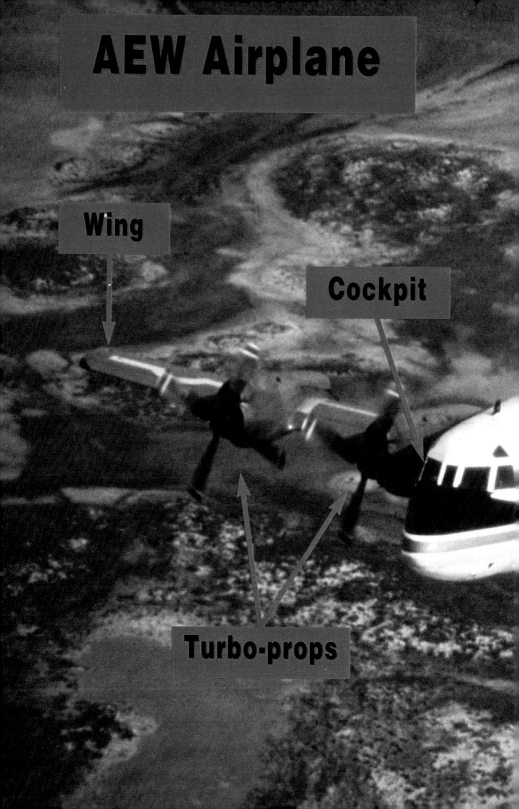

AEW Airplane

Wing

Cockpit

Turbo-props

Radar Dish

Tail

Turbo-props

Chapter 5

Weapons and Equipment

Customs Service officers use different kinds of weapons and equipment. The weapons and equipment help make their jobs easier and safer.

Weapons

Sometimes Customs Service officers use weapons to protect themselves and the public. They also use weapons to stop and capture violent suspects. Violent means likely to harm others.

Customs Service officers use their least powerful weapons first. These weapons disable suspects without killing them. These weapons include pepper spray. Pepper spray causes a burning feeling in the eyes and the lungs. Customs

Sometimes Customs Service officers use weapons to protect themselves and the public.

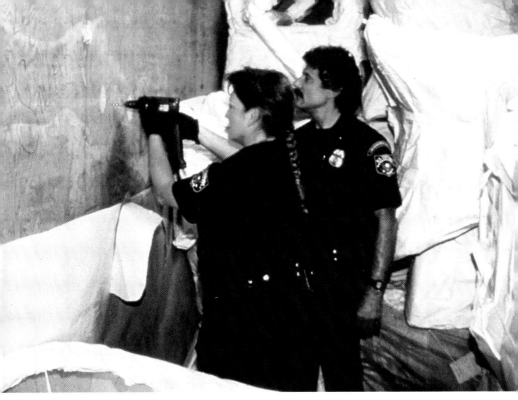

Customs Service inspectors wear blue uniforms with patches and badges on them.

Service officers use pepper spray to disable suspects without using their guns.

All customs officers carry semiautomatic handguns. Semiautomatic handguns are powerful handguns that fire bullets quickly. The handguns are short-range weapons. Semiautomatic handguns hold 14 to 17 rounds. A round is a bullet.

Sometimes agents need semiautomatic rifles to defend themselves and fight with smugglers. The

M-16 is the most common semiautomatic rifle agents use.

The M-16 is light. This makes it easy to carry and use. The M-16's range is 600 yards (546 meters). Each M-16 holds up to 30 rounds.

Uniforms

Customs Service officers wear different uniforms. The uniforms help people, police, and other officers see them. This reduces the chances of accidental shootings.

Inspectors wear blue uniforms or blue uniforms with white shirts. The uniforms also have patches and badges on them. They show that inspectors have the authority to ask questions, search property, and make arrests.

Many agents also wear uniforms. But sometimes agents do not want to be identified. They wear camouflage uniforms for some operations. Camouflage is coloring that blends in with the surroundings. Many camouflage uniforms are green and brown. These uniforms help agents hide from smugglers.

Other agents do not wear uniforms. They wear street clothes. Street clothes help agents pretend to be ordinary people during undercover operations.

Armored Vests and Shields

Customs Service officers wear armored vests when they may be facing gunfire. Armor is a protective metal or plastic covering. Armored vests can protect agents and officers from some gunshots.

Sometimes agents and officers also use shields. The shields are made of lightweight armor. They provide added protection against gunshots and small explosions.

Computers and Other Devices

Customs Service officers rely on computers. Computers help them keep track of goods, identify smugglers, and communicate with each other. Communicate means to share information through written or spoken means.

X-ray machines help Customs Service officers quickly check mail, baggage, shipping containers, and trucks. An X-ray machine uses special beams of light to take pictures of the insides of objects. Objects range from packages to shipping containers. X-ray pictures give officers clues about what is inside the objects.

Customs Service officers also use sniffers. A sniffer is a hand-held device that can detect some

Inspectors use X-ray machines to check baggage.

scents. Customs Service officers use sniffers to search for drugs in automobiles and on people.

The Best Defense

Smugglers make billions of dollars bringing illegal goods into the United States. They break the law by avoiding tariffs. The goods they bring into the country harm the public.

But the smuggling problem would be much worse without Customs Service officers. They provide the best defense against smugglers. Each day officers and agents risk their lives to shut down smuggling activities.

Words to Know

agent (AY-juhnt)—a high-ranking law enforcement officer

armor (AR-mur)—a protective metal or plastic covering

commando group (kuh-MAN-doh GROOP)—a heavily armed assault team

detect (di-TEKT)—to notice or discover something

enforce (en-FORSS)—to make sure that laws are obeyed

foreign (FOR-uhn)—from another country

infrared system (in-fruh-RED SISS-tuhm)—machinery that detects objects by the heat they give off

inspector (in-SPEK-tur)—a person who checks or searches things

interceptor (in-tur-SEP-tur)—a speedboat built to catch and stop other boats

interdiction (in-tur-DIK-shun)—the act of stopping an illegal activity

investigate (in-VESS-tuh-gate)—gathering facts to discover who committed a crime

maintain (mayn-TAYN)—to keep something in good condition

monitor (MON-uh-tur)—to watch closely

pepper spray (PEP-ur SPRAY)—a spray that causes a burning feeling in the eyes and the lungs

port of entry (PORT UHV EN-tree)—a controlled place where people and goods enter a country

radar (RAY-dar)—machinery that sends out radio waves to locate and guide things

revenue (REV-uh-noo)—money raised from tariffs and other taxes

smuggler (SMUHG-lur)—a person who sneaks illegal goods into or out of a country

tariff (TA-rif)—a tax on goods entering a country

turbo-prop engine (TUR-boh-prop EN-juhn)—a jet engine that turns a propeller

To Learn More

Cohen, Paul and Shari Cohen. *Careers in Law Enforcement and Security*. New York: Rosen Publishing Group, 1995.

George, Charles and Linda George. *Police Dogs*. Mankato, Minn.: RiverFront Books, 1998.

Green, Michael. *Bomb Detection Squads*. Mankato, Minn.: RiverFront Books, 1998.

Ring, Elizabeth. *Detector Dogs: Hot on the Scent*. Brookfield, Conn.: Millbrook Press, 1993.

Useful Addresses

Air Interdiction Division
The U.S. Customs Service
Air Interdiction Division
1300 Pennsylvania Avenue NW
Washington, DC 20229

Customs National Aviation Center
5020 South Meridian Avenue
Oklahoma City, OK 73119

The U.S. Customs Service
Office of Public Affairs
c/o Department of the Treasury
Washington, DC 20229-0001

Internet Sites

DEA Home Page
http://www.usdoj.gov/dea/index.htm

The Department of Treasury Kids' Page
http://www.ustreas.gov/treasury/kids/

U.S. Customs Service Home Page
http://www.customs.treas.gov

Customs Service officers provide the best defense against smugglers.

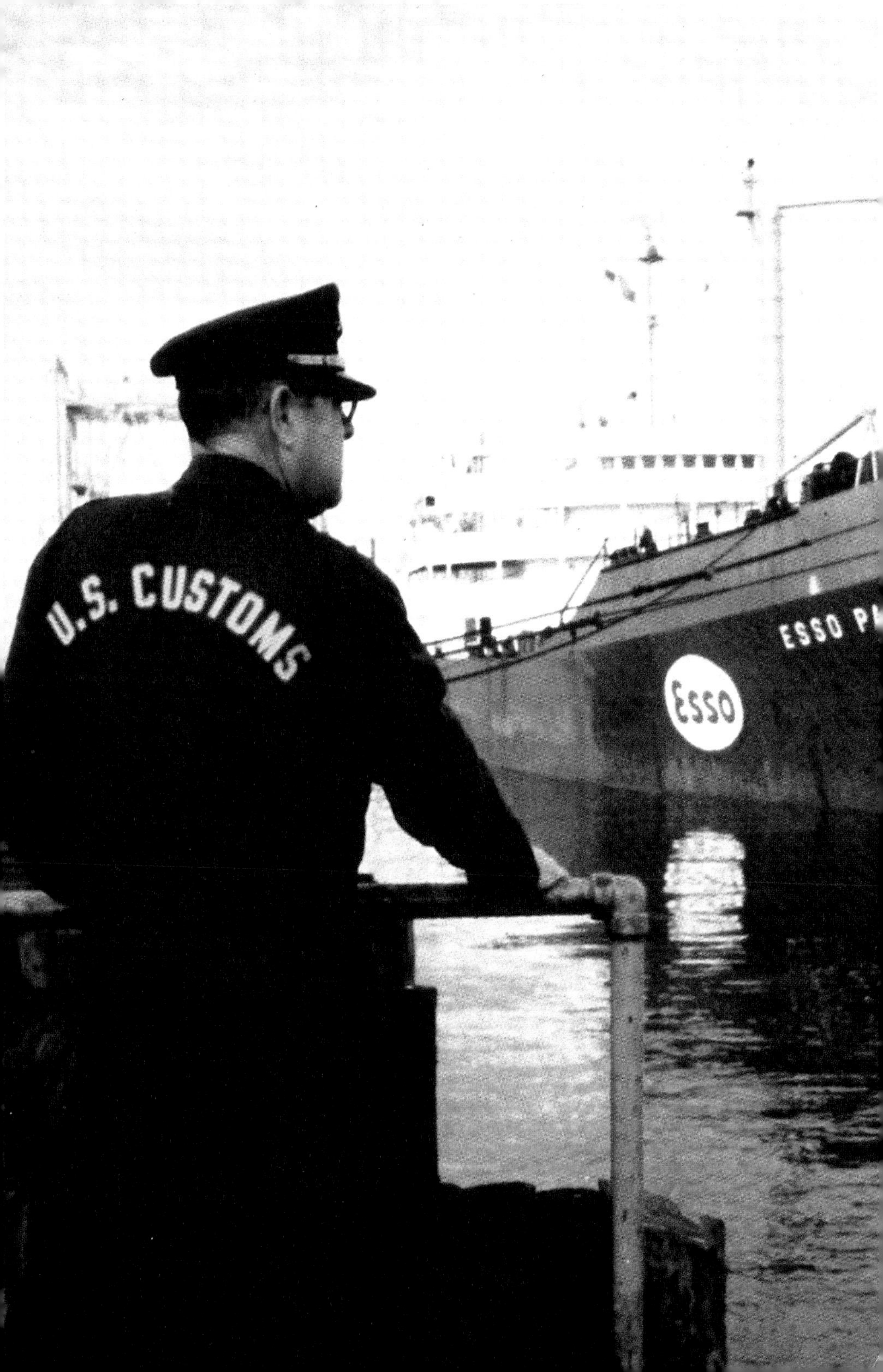
U.S. CUSTOMS
ESSO
Esso

Index